a record of
my remnants

Katie Hulme

Translated by Oul Han

MOONRISE
Meanjin, Australia

a record of
my remnants

ISBN 978-0-6450486-8-1 (paperback)
ISBN 978-0-6450486-9-8 (eBook)

Cover design by Alexander Coolican
Typeset by Alexander Coolican
Edited by Nikola Champlin
Translated by Oul Han

First published in 2021

Moonrise
Meanjin, Australia
www.moonrise.revolutionaries.com.au

Related titles from Moonrise

Through the darkness, I will love myself edited by Wallea Eaglehawk, Nikola Champlin & Padya Paramita

To Stephen (let's never take our twisted red parabola for granted),
Jess (with whom I share mutual fractures),
my Dad (a kindred spirit whose passion for the pen helped reignite my own),
and the odd souls who process life better through poetry than prose (thank you
for reminding me that that's okay).

Contents

interlude: god of the gap

Contents

jachin and boaz (야긴과 보아스)

outro: come with me

preface

2019 was a year that will remain, for me, forever bookended by two oddly shaped pillars of grief. A year of personal trials that would soon be dwarfed by a pandemic of global proportions. My best friend knew my path; her miscarriage was tattooed on the side of her finger. Me, I sought solace in another form of ink. I wonder if we all need something permanent to claim those pillars as our own.

The poems of this book are arranged in chronological order. There is no theme to tie them all together, other than the linear experience of the poet. Yet this story is far from linear—for it ends, in many ways, back where it began: the empty pages of a partially filled journal, bound in a cheap replica of van Gogh's *The Bedroom*.

While the poems in "jachin and boaz" and "outro: come with me" have been revised and rewritten many a time, the works in "intro: let me in" and "ode to the west wind" remain unaltered, transcribed from their original hand-written versions where they had waited, preserved and unread, for almost two decades between the covers of my journal. The titles, however, have been assigned retrospectively. I distinctly remember the memories attached to some of my words, but not all of them. I wrote them, and yet I felt like changing them now would be putting words into someone else's mouth. So instead of twisting them to say what I wish to say now, I wanted to let the 'me' of then have a chance to speak, too.

I am, at this stage of my life, both a wife and a mother. For a long time, I feared putting pen to paper. The words that do not exist ("interlude: god of the gap") are also a part of this story. Despite the predominance of these roles in my life, you will note that they are not the focus of the latter half of this book.

Not because they are not important to me, nor because I do not draw strength and joy from these parts of my life, but because I needed a moment to explore who I am apart from those roles so that I could bring more than just a derivative self to the people who matter to me most. In the process of putting myself together, I found a piece of myself that I forgot was missing, and for that I will forever be grateful.

This book is very much a confession of catharsis, and an exploration of the lines between escapism and immersion, passion and addiction, joy and idolatry. My written words have always been a bit selfish, but I hope that by sharing this collection of my "thorns," at least one of you may find comfort, and these words of mine may become just a little bit less selfish.

Katie West Hulme
2020.10.27
Born 1985

on translation

You might be wondering why this book has been translated into Korean and published in a bilingual format. The reason is three-fold. First, my journey in the second half of this book was aided, or perhaps accompanied, by music sung in Korean, a language that is not my own. These foreign words weren't merely a soundtrack, however, but rather an art form with which I engaged, interacted, and healed. So publishing in both English and Korean is, in part, a tribute.

Second, while there is something to be said for carefully crafted words—and there is no doubt that nuances of meaning, rhyme, and meter are sometimes lost in translation—there is also something to be said for engaging with something that you don't fully understand. How well it rolls off the tongue becomes less important than what it means, and there is joy to be found in the process of attempting to appreciate it, however imperfectly. I hope to pass this small gift to at least one of my readers. If anything, you might experience my words in an unadulterated form through the Korean translation—less eloquent, but more raw.

Lastly, when translating into Korean, the relationships between speaker, subject, and listener are crucial in a way they are not in the English language. Korean speech levels, honorifics, and pronouns capture nuances which are not directly expressed in English. At the crux of my writing is a dialogue, so perhaps, too, having my work translated would introduce questions I have been itching to have raised.

from the translator

This book of poetry stands out by showing the English original and the Korean translation right next to each other. For the translator, this is an interesting setting. It differs from the usual custom, namely, to only show the translated result to the readers. In comparison, showing the original and translation together is, in some sense, ballsy. The reason is that the translator's interpretation is laid completely bare, including her judgments and word choices.

Arguably, this effect is even greater for the format of poetry, as opposed to novels or essays. The format of poetry extends the playing field of interpretive options, on which the poem stands and artfully balances vagueness and ambiguity. In this sense, I felt that the work of translation is a combination of at least two aspects. On the one hand, translation is an art because it holds subjective interpretations. On the other hand, it is a professional skill, aimed at matching words and expressions that are most adequate from an objective standpoint. In any case, I hope that my work preserves the author's intentions in the best way.

Specific to the Korean language, I have steered away from honorifics as much as possible, striving for a smoother and more modern style instead. I only used it for a couple of poems where the context seemed especially appropriate. Further, changing the order of sentence parts was sometimes crucial for the content delivery, so I changed the order of lines in some cases.

One of the last poems in this book, "carrying joy" in part four, is one of the only ones that rhyme. It follows the rhyming scheme of A-B-C-B and arranges words in a rhythm, like a song lyric. To transpose this trait as much as possible, I applied the Korean rhyming theory that is the unique achievement of Korean Hip-hop and rap (without it, systematic notions of Korean rhyming would not exist). This is a novel and unconventional approach for poetry translation into Korean. I hope this is an additional subtlety that the author and the readers can enjoy.

번역사의 메시지

이 시집의 독특한 점은 영어 원문과 한글 번역이 나란히 있다는 사실입니다. 번역사에게는 흥미로운 설정입니다. 책 번역이 의례 그렇듯이 번역된 결과물만을 독자에게 보여주는 것이 아니기 때문입니다. 그에 비해 원문과 번역을 둘 다 보여준다는 것은 어떻게 보면 용감합니다. 원어를 어떻게 해석했는지, 어떤 판단을 내리고 어떤 단어를 골랐는지 고스란히 나타나니까요.

소설이나 수필이 아닌, 시의 형식이라서 더 그렇습니다. 시의 형식이란 해석의 여지가 더 넓어진 초원 위에서, 아련하고 애매하게 줄타기하는 예술이어서 더 그렇습니다. 그러한 해석의 다양성은 제 번역을 통해서 더 넓어지기도, 더 좁아지기도 한 것을 느꼈습니다. 이런 의미에서 번역이라는 작업이 적어도 두 가지 측면의 결합이라고 느꼈습니다. 한 편으로는 다분히 주관적인 해석이 흘러 들어가는 예술이자, 다른 한 편으로는 객관적으로 가장 적합한 단어와 표현을 조합하려는 전문 기술입니다. 아무쪼록 작가님의 의도가 잘 전달되었으면 좋겠습니다.

부드럽고 현대적으로 읽히기 위해 존칭은 최대한 생략하였고, 해당 시의 맥락에 어울린다고 판단될 때에만 사용하였습니다. 또한, 내용 전달을 위해 어순이 중요할 때가 있어서, 원문의 줄 순서를 바꾸는 기법을 조금씩 사용하였습니다.

4장의 마무리를 장식하는 "carrying joy" (기쁨을 지니다) 라는 시는 이 시집에서는 드물게 라이밍의 구조를 띱니다. A-B-C-B 로 이루어졌고 운율 또한 노랫말처럼 짰습니다. 이러한 특징을 최대한 살리기 위해 한국 힙합과 랩 고유의 라이밍 이론을 적용해서 번역했습니다. 이런 색다르고 독보적인 시도가 이 시집의 작가님과 독자분께 또 하나의 묘미이길 바랍니다.

intro: let me in

서문: 날 들여보내 줘

supplication

A whisper in the wind and I wonder—
voices in the distance wind their way up the stairs,
and I wait.
Caught between realities,
I don't know where I am.

My fist pounds on your door—
my arm is tired but you do not come.
Enticement—meant to drag me away,
I dig my heels in,
yet you do not come to my aid.

In a way, your gift of freedom is poisonous—
I fear I will turn the other way,
unable to resist,
and you will not step in.

So I worry,
as I watch the rain on the windowpane,
and I pray you'll open the door.

2001.07.02

간구

바람 속의 속삭임, 궁금증이 인다—
머나먼 여럿의 목소리가 계단을 타고 오르고,
나는 기다린다.
현실 사이에 갇혀서
내가 어디에 있는지 모른다.

내 주먹이 너의 문을 때린다.
내 팔은 지쳤어도 너는 오지 않는다.
유혹—나를 끌고 가기 위함,
나는 발 뒤꿈치를 더 깊게 박지만
너는 나를 도우려 오지 않는다.

네가 준 자유라는 선물은 어쩌면 독극물—
나는 내가 고개를 돌릴까봐 두렵다,
저항하지 못할까봐,
그래서 네가 들어오지 않을까봐.

그래서 나는 걱정한다,
창문의 빗물을 바라보며,
네가 문을 열기를 기도한다.

2001.07.02

ode to the west wind

서풍을 위한 헌정 시

nightscape

If thou hast never tried to touch the stars
and fallen when your reach was still too short,
thou hast not loved.

And if thou-st never tried to see beyond
the veil that hides the light within the dark,
thou hast not loved.

If thou hast never seen the crack that breaks it,
the grains of sand that dare to rub it raw,
the heat that stifles deep the heart within it,
thou hast not loved.

And if thou cannot-st find a way to catch,
the stars within their distant moonlit veil,
the ladder to the sky you still must find,
or thou hast not loved.

2002.09.02

야경

별을 만지기 위해 당신의 손을 뻗은 적이 없다면
거리가 아직 미처 닿지 못해서 추락한 적이 없다면
당신은 사랑한 적이 없느니라.

그리고 암흑 속의 불빛을 가리는 베일의
너머로 더 멀리 보려 한 적이 없다면
당신은 사랑한 적이 없느니라.

그것을 깨뜨리는 균열
그것에 감히 생채기를 내려 하는 모래알
그 안의 심장을 깊게 억누르는 그것을 본 적이 없다면
당신은 사랑한 적이 없느니라.

그리고 머나먼 달빛 뒤에 가려진 별을
따오기 위한 방도를 찾을 수 없다 해도
하늘로 가는 사다리는 찾아야만 함이라
그렇지 않다면 당신은 사랑한 적이 없느니라.

2002.09.02

terrarium

I am bent,
arms hover awkwardly,
as I tap;
One, two, three seeds—
no—more than that.
I jerk, to stop the cascade,
then proceed to tap... and tap.

In the mirrors,
I can see myself from all sides,
and I observe myself,
as I imagine another might.
I wonder what I look like,
to this outside world
that I can never access?
Because we are all trapped
in the confines of our singular minds.

I stop this train of thought,
because it always leads to a feeling
of incredible insignificance.
Right now,
I am alone and important
in my world of potted plants.

I am free to dream,
to fantasise without prying eyes.
I am allowed to wander
and to entertain,
as long as I don't forget
where my seeds have fallen.

2003.10.29

테라리움

나는 구부정하고
팔을 어색하게 든 채로
두드린다:
씨앗 한 개, 두 개, 세 개—
더는 안돼.
쏟아지지 않게끔 난 멈칫하고
다시 두드리길 시작하고... 또 두드린다.

거울을 보면
나 자신을 여러 측면에서 바라볼 수 있다.
그렇게 나를 관찰한다,
남이 나를 볼 법한 시야로.
내가 절대 들어가지 못할
외부 세상의 눈에 비친
나의 모습이 어떨지 궁금하다.
우리는 모두 갇혀있기 때문이다
개별적 머릿속 생각의 한계 속에.

이런 상상의 나래를 이내 그만둔다.
언제나 결국 느끼게 될 것은
엄청난 초라함이기에.
지금, 이 순간
나는 혼자고 나는 중요하다
화분으로 이루어진 내 세상 속에서.

나는 자유롭게 꿈꿀 수 있고
따가운 눈초리 없이 상상할 수 있다.
나는 떠돌아다닐 수 있고
생각을 펼칠 수 있다,
내 씨앗이 어디에 떨어졌는지
내가 망각하지만 않는다면.

2003.10.29

commute

Silence,
as we sit,
eyes roaming across the floor,
over the plastic seats,
and out the window.

Darkness has fallen
as our reflections stare back at us.
We watch ourselves sway
and jerk over the potholes;
hands folded,
or wrapped around the cool metal of support.

Words and thoughts
evade our grasp,
until our glazed expressions
are broken
by the stop.

2003.11.02

출퇴근

침묵,
우리는 앉았고
눈은 바닥 위를 맴돌고
플라스틱 의자를 훑고
창밖으로 움직인다.

어둠이 이르렀으며
우리의 반사된 형상이 우리를 노려본다.
우리 자신들이 흔들리는 것과
틈새 위를 지날 때 덜컹거림을 본다;
손을 포개거나
차가운 금속 지지대에 감은 채로.

말과 생각은
우리의 통제를 떠나고,
멍한 우리의 표정이
깨지는 순간은
정거할 때.

2003.11.02

look away

We crunch along the gravel path,
feet clomp in unison,
and I am aware
of being alone
in this crowd.
Headphones and silence mark division
within conformity,
as we all let our eyes
slide conveniently away
from the oncoming soul
who threatens to make contact
and shatter the spell.

2003.11.05

눈을 돌리다

우리는 자갈길 위를 자박자박 걸으며
우리의 발걸음은 동시에 뚜벅뚜벅하고,
나는 잘 알고 있다
혼자라는 걸
이 무리 속에서.
헤드폰과 침묵은 우리를 명백히 나누지만
그것은 순응 속에서 이루어지고,
우리는 모두 눈을
편안한 곳으로 돌려서
다가오는 영혼을 피한다
접촉으로 우리를 위협하고
마법 주문을 깨 버릴 영혼을.

2003.11.05

never was

There's a feeling I want to capture on paper,
the disappointment at the absence
of something that never was.

But it takes too long
to processes this sensation,
and I am falling asleep.

2003.11.22

한번도

서면으로 남기고 싶은 느낌이 있다
한번도 존재하지 않았던 어떤 무엇의
부재를 향한 실망.

하지만 이 느낌을 정리하는 것이
너무 오래 걸려서
이제는 잠에 든다.

2003.11.22

box blind

I carried a special box.

Her eyes saw red,
his eyes saw blue,
her eyes saw cracks,
his eyes saw holes.

Red, blue, cracks, and holes
were all there—
but it broke my heart
to realise they didn't see the box.

2004.01.01

상자를 못보다

나는 특별한 상자를 쥐었다.

그녀의 눈은 붉은색을 보고
그의 눈은 푸른색을 보았고
그녀의 눈은 균열을 보고
그의 눈은 구멍을 보았다.

붉은색, 푸른색, 균열, 구멍은 모두
실제로 있었다—
하지만 내가 정말 가슴 아팠던 이유는
그들이 상자를 못 본다는 걸 깨달아서이다.

2004.01.01

speech blanket

She lay next to me,
her bony fingers clutching my arm,
her soft voice cut into the night.
She spoke to herself,
as she told me he was scared.

He told me tonight that he didn't want to die,
he's been leaving the lights on at night,
I should have known.

I am silent and wait.

He is a good man at heart, you know?

I know.
Her voice is earnest,
laced with pain and regret,
for harsh words spoken in the past.

And so I let her tell me
what she needs to hear.

2004.01.01

말의 담요

그녀는 내 옆에 누워있었고,
그녀의 깡마른 손가락은 내 팔을 거머쥔 채였고
그녀의 부드러운 목소리는 밤을 깨웠다.
그녀는 혼잣말하면서도
두렵다고 나에게 말했다.

그는 죽고 싶지 않다고 오늘 밤 내게 말했다
그는 밤마다 불빛을 켜놓고 지내왔다
난 왜 몰랐을까.

나는 조용히 기다린다.

그는 사실 마음이 선한 사람이거든, 알아?

난 안다.
그녀의 목소리는 진지하고,
과거에 뱉은 모진 말에 대한
아픔과 후회가 가미되었다.

그래서 나는 잠자코 들어주었다
그녀가 듣기 원하는 말을 나에게 말하게끔.

2004.01.01

when years grow heavy

She wears her age
in the elegant tremble of her hands.
You can read the effort of every movement,
yet her eyes dare you to insult her dignity.

She mostly just sits,
wrestling with fatigue and denying the pain.
She loses herself in a world of silence,
her hearing unable to catch the subtleties.

It would be easy to mistake age as stupidity,
to miss the wisdom
in her breath of a voice.
But I know better,
and I marvel
at the woman beneath all those years.

2004.01.01

세월이 무거워질 때

그녀는 세월을
손의 우아한 떨림 위에 걸친다.
동작 하나하나의 힘겨움이 전해지지만
그녀의 눈동자는 그녀의 품위를 모욕하게 두지 않는다.

그녀는 거의 앉아만 있다,
피로와 싸우며 고통을 부인한 채로.
그녀는 침묵의 세상 속에서 길을 잃고
그녀의 청각은 미세함을 감지하지 못한다.

고령을 아둔함으로 착각하기는 쉽다,
숨결 같은 그녀의 목소리 속
지혜를 놓치는 것도.
하지만 제대로 알고 있는 나는
감탄한다
그 모든 세월 아래 놓인 여성에 대하여.

2004.01.01

to cauterise

There was joy the other day,
a fellowship that made all else fade.
I savoured it,
but I didn't share it.

Why do I burn the pain
so deep into my memory,
and let the joy fade into the forgotten?
Who am I, to reject it so?

2004.01.01

지지다

최근에 기쁨을 느꼈다,
모든 것을 희미하게 만들던 유대감을.
난 그것을 음미했지만
나누지는 않았다.

왜 나는 내 기억 속에
고통을 깊게 지지고
기쁨이 망각 속으로 사라지게 놔뒀을까?
내가 뭐라고 그것을 그토록 거부했을까?

2004.01.01

to quench

It is a moment
of peaceful intimacy,
where all else seems insignificant.

Curled beneath the covers,
scribbling beneath the dimness of a single light,
I embrace the stillness of early morning
that bids me sleep.

This thirst could keep me up all night,
but I know a single night
could not quench this.

No,
I long for that day,
when my joy shall be complete,
and my thirst,
quenched for eternity.

2004.01.01

갈증을 풀다

평화로운 친밀감의
순간이다,
다른 모든 것이 보잘것없어질 만큼의.

이불 아래 웅크려서,
작은 불빛의 침침함 속에서 끄적이며,
나에게 잠을 건네는
이른 아침의 고요함을 반긴다.

이 갈증은 나를 밤새 잠 못 이루게도 하지만,
하룻밤 따위로는
풀리지 않을 거란 것을 안다.

그래,
그날을 고대한다,
내 기쁨이 완전해질 때를,
그리고 내 갈증이,
영원히 풀릴 때를.

2004.01.01

the truth told

To be told the unknown truth
may cut,
but opened eyes are grateful.

It is when you are told the truth you know,
the truth that eats at your soul,
that weakens you even when you face it head-on,
and you look at the truth-bearers eyes
that dismiss you as blind,
it is then that the truth no longer heals.

I want to burn those eyes
for reminding me.

2004.04.28

솔직히 말하면

모르던 사실을 남에게서 듣는 것은
아프지만,
열린 눈은 감사함으로 가득하다.

하지만 이미 아는 사실을 남에게서 들었을 때,
그것이 내 영혼을 갉아먹는 사실일 때,
그것을 아무리 정면 돌파해도 나의 약점일 때,
그리고 진실 전달자의 눈을 보았더니
나를 아둔하다고 깎아내리고 있음을 알아차릴 때,
그때의 진실은 치유를 선사하지 않는다.

나는 그 눈을 불태우고 싶다
나를 기억하게 했기에.

2004.04.28

bloodshot

Is it hard to look them in the eyes
and know that they're naïve?
Is it hard to shake their hands and smile
when you know that they are blind?

Or, do you take comfort
in their world of innocence?
Is it possible to return,
to partake,
when tainted?
Or does the blood in your eyes
drain into your soul?

2004.04.28

핏발

그들의 눈을 똑바로 바라보며
그들의 순진함을 견뎌내기란 어려울까?
그들이 못 본다는 사실을 알면서도
그들과 악수하며 미소 짓기란 어려울까?

혹은 그들의 순진무구한 세상으로 인한
위로로 삼게 될까?
때가 묻은 이상
참여하거나
돌아가기란 가능할까?
혹은 네 눈의 피가
네 영혼 속으로 흘러내려갈까?

2004.04.28

to touch a sound

Their voices echo off the stone archways,
and I imagine I hear heaven,
a beauty that urges me to contemplate
moments of forever.
And my sense of self
begins to fade into broken insignificance.
I long to cling and not return,
embrace the echo and capture it in my heart.

2005.04.11

소리를 만지다

그들의 목소리는 돌로 된 아치형 입구에 반사되고
천국의 소리가 들리는 듯한 상상과
어떤 아름다움이 나를 생각에 잠기게 한다
영원의 순간들에 대해.
그리고 내 자아감은
부서진 초라함 속으로 사라진다.
나는 매달리되 돌아가지 안고 싶고,
메아리를 끌어안고 내 마음속에 간직하고프다.

2005.04.11

house of mirrors

There are too many mirrors in this house.

I don't know which is worse,
the mirror that tells me I'm beautiful,
or the mirror that taunts me with all of my imperfections.
Oh, that vanity and self-contempt are one in the same,
though their lies are ever conflicting.

I wish these mirrors would disappear,
that my eyes would not be tempted
to look into them again and again.

2005.05.24

거울의 집

이 집에는 거울이 너무 많다.

뭐가 더 최악인지 모르겠다
내가 아름답다고 해주는 거울이,
혹은 나의 모든 부족함을 조롱하는 거울이.
오, 저 허영심과 자기혐오는 동일한 하나지만,
그들의 거짓말은 영원히 충돌한다.

저 거울들이 사라졌으면 한다,
내 눈이 시험에 들지 않아서
그들을 다시금 또 다시금 응시하지 않도록.

2005.05.24

a record of my remnants

And there will be no record of these thoughts tonight.
Yet, these words spoken to you,
in the silence of my heart,
have been heard.

2005.06.08

내 그루터기의 기록

하여서 오늘 밤의 이런 생각들을 기록하지 않으려다.
하지만 너에게 건넨 이 말들은
내 마음의 침묵 속에서
들렸다.

2005.06.08

interlude: god of the gap

막간: 틈새의 신

jachin and boaz

야긴과 보아스

tea on a cold night | 야긴

Etching sincerity into a page used to be easy.
But age has clouded transparency,
even—no, especially—with myself.
Shall I be honest once again?
You let me hear your story,
so I will let you hear mine.

I guard two beautiful lives,
but the third is slipping away.
They are worth more than many sparrows—
yet we fly while their wings are ruthlessly plucked.
My body kills them slowly,
without asking my permission.
Speed and certainty would be a blessing.

To save or be saved,
sometimes it's not up to us.

I hate myself for the lack of tears.
I'm just fine,
but wish nothing more than to admit that I am not.
Is it still pain in the absence of emotion?
I'd rather be sad than numb.
I'd rather be weak than cold.

Mutual fractures weld unbreakable bonds—
yes,
good can indeed be forged from night;
but don't credit darkness with the light that pierces it.

Sometimes there is no reason;
just admit that this world is broken,
and take joy in that which remains un-shattered.

추운 밤의 차 | 야긴

진정성을 종이 한 장에 새기는 일이 한때는 쉬웠다.
하지만 나이가 드니 투명성이 뿌예졌고
심지어–아니, 특히나–나에 대해서 그렇다.
다시 솔직해져 볼까?
넌 너의 이야기를 내게 들려줬으니,
내 이야기도 이제 네게 들려줘야지.

난 두 개의 아름다운 인생을 지켜내지만
세 번째는 떠나가려고 한다.
그들은 여러 참새보다 가치 있지만—
우리가 날아다니는 동안 그들의 날개깃은 무자비하게 뽑힌다.
내 몸은 그들을 천천히 죽이며
내 허락을 맡지도 않는다.
속도와 확실성이란 축복일 터.

구원하는 것과 구원 받는 것은
가끔은 우리에게 달려 있지 않다.

눈물이 부족한 나 자신이 밉다.
난 그래도 괜찮다
하지만 괜찮지 않다고 인정하고픈 마음이 무엇보다 간절하다.
감정이 메말랐다면 이걸 고통이라 부를 수 있을까?
난 무덤덤하기보단 슬프길 택하겠다.
난 냉담하기보단 나약하길 택하겠다.

상호적 골절은 견고한 결합을 용접한다—
그래,
밤을 벼려서 선함을 만들어낼 수 있다만;
어두움을 뚫는 빛이 어두움의 업적은 아니다.

가끔은 아무 이유가 없다;
그저 이 세상이 망가졌음을 인정하고
아직 온전한 채인 것들을 즐거워하라.

In a brief moment of happiness,
guilt and thankfulness compete.
But thankfulness brings the tears I've so desperately craved,
and I am relieved to let them fall.

So to you I am grateful,
for gently wrapping
my fingers
around this mug.
It doesn't fix anything,
but it's warm.

2019.05.03

행복한 순간의 찰나에
죄책감과 감사함이 서로 경쟁한다.
하지만 감사함은 내가 그토록 갈망하던 눈물을 동반하고
떨어지는 눈물에 나는 안도감을 느낀다.

그래서 너에게 난 감사하다
내 손가락을
이 머그잔에
부드럽게 감싸게 해줘서.
이것은 아무것도 해결해주지 않지만
적어도 따듯하니까.

2019.05.03

overflow

We used to talk all the time—
a continuous stream of consciousness,
leaking from my pen.

I stopped talking, you kept listening.

This empty page feels vast after such a long pause,
but it is probably miniscule in your eyes.

I often wonder why you've been so good to me.
Blessings keep falling, undeserved,
despite my silence.

To whom much has been given, much will be required,
so I wonder what is expected of me.

I can at least take joy,
but surely that is not enough?

Then again,
if I cannot even do that well, how shall I do more?

So,
teach me joy,
teach me thankfulness,
teach me to delight,
until my cup overflows.

흘러넘친

우리는 항상 대화를 나누곤 했다—
의식의 지속적인 흐름이
내 펜에서 흐르듯이.

나는 대화를 멈췄고 당신은 계속 경청했다.

오랜 정지 후의 빈 페이지는 거대하게 느껴지지만
아마 당신 눈에는 매우 작아 보일 것이다.

왜 당신은 나에게 그토록 잘 해주었는지 종종 궁금하다.
축복은 계속 쏟아 내려서 과분하다
내가 침묵했음에도 불구하고 받은 것이라.

많은 것을 받은 사람에게 많은 것을 요구해야 할 것이니
나에게 무엇을 요구할지 궁금하다.

적어도 기쁨을 누릴 수는 있겠건만
설마 그걸로 충분하지는 않겠지?

하지만 다른 한편으로는,
내가 그것도 못 한다면 그 이상을 해낼 수나 있을까?

그러니까
내게 기쁨을 가르쳐 주소서
내게 감사함을 가르쳐 주소서
내게 환희를 가르쳐 주소서
내 컵이 흘러넘칠 때까지.

And as it runs over,
perhaps these blessings will spill onto another.
I hope this to be true.
Because I fear—
no—
I know,
they are wasted,
just sitting in my cup.

2019.04.18

그리고 흘러넘칠 적에
이 모든 축복이 다른 컵으로 흐를지도 모른다.
그랬으면 좋겠다.
왜냐하면, 내가 걱정하는 바는—
아니—
확신하는 바는
이건 축복의 낭비라는 것
내 컵에 그저 담겨만 있다면.

2019.04.18

the cause of my euphoria

Not long ago,
my soul was dry.
Numb.
Cold.
But right now,
the joy is unparalleled.

I fear joy has transitioned to euphoria,
and euphoria cannot last.
Be joyful always, not euphoric.

How did you turn a cold night into morning so quickly?
This sunrise is spectacular, and I never even asked for it.

How does someone undeserving,
gracefully receive a gift?
I shall not hand it back—
surely that would offend you, the giver.

Whatever is true,
whatever is noble,
whatever is lovely,
you told me to think about such things—
and right now, they are intoxicating.
Should I be wary—
or is this what living feels like?

2019.05.07

내 희열의 원인

얼마 전에
내 영혼은 메말라 있었다.
마비된 채로.
차가운 채로.
하지만 지금은
내 기쁨에 견줄 만할 것이 없다.

걱정이다, 기쁨이 희열로 변했을까 봐,
희열은 오래 가지 못하니까.
항상 기뻐하라, 하지만 희열에 휩쓸리지 말아라.

어떻게 당신은 이토록 빠르게, 추운 밤을 아침으로 변하게 했는지?
해돋이는 장관을 이루는데 나는 이걸 간청한 적조차 없다.

이렇게도 부족한 사람인데 어찌하여
선물을 은혜롭게 받았을까?
다시 돌려드리지 않을 것이다—
이걸 내게 준 당신에게 모욕이 될 테니.

참된 모든 것과
고결한 모든 것과
사랑스러운 모든 것,
이런 것을 생각하라고 당신은 내게 말했다—
그리고 현재로서는 난 그것에 취한다.
경계해야 할까—
혹은 이것이야말로 살아있다는 기분일까?

2019.05.07

remembrance

My memories are loose threads
in a fragile tapestry.
If I want to bind my pattern to that of yours,
then we should weave these threads together
and tighten the knots with words.

2019.06.19

추억

내 기억은 취약한 융단 속
헐거운 실 같다.
내가 나의 무늬를 너의 무늬에 묶고자 한다면
우리는 이 실을 하나로 엮어야 할 것이고
매듭을 단어로 꼬아야 할 것이다.

2019.06.19

suffocating sun

Moonchild,
you suffer beneath the sun,
but the moon—

                              the moon is bearable.

You can stare at the moon
without burning your eyes—

                              the moon is gentle.

The night may be dark,
but it is not without light—

                    yes child, the moon is kind.

Yet the sun reappears,
casting a shadow
as you attempt to face it—

                              oh, the sun is blinding.

Turn around, Dear Moonchild,
and greet your shadow
so you no longer need to shield your eyes,
for the sun—

                              the sun is bearable.

2019.06.19

질식하는 태양

달의 아이야,
넌 태양 아래서 고통받지만
달은—

$\qquad\qquad\qquad\qquad$ 달은 견딜 만 하단다.

네가 달을 뚫어지게 보아도
눈이 타들어 가지 않아—

$\qquad\qquad\qquad\qquad$ 달은 온화하단다.

밤은 어두울지 몰라도
빛을 함께 지녔다—

$\qquad\qquad\qquad$ 그래, 아이야, 달은 다정하단다.

하지만 태양은 다시 등장하고
그늘을 드리우고
너는 그걸 마주 보려 해본다—

$\qquad\qquad\qquad\qquad$ 오, 태양은 눈 부시다.

친애하는 달의 아이야, 뒤돌아봐,
네 그림자에 인사해봐
네 눈을 이제는 가릴 필요 없게
왜냐하면 태양은—

$\qquad\qquad\qquad\qquad$ 태양은 견딜 만 하단다.

2019.06.19

constraints without determinism

We must each operate within our own constraints,
binding conditions in a multi-variable equation—
our fates restricted to a continuous surface,
a multiplicity of solutions.

And the intersection of you and me,
cannot be described by a singular point,
but rather,
a winding red thread,
a twisted parabola,
connecting my plane to yours.

2019.08.10

결정론 없는 제약

우리는 각자의 제약 내에서 각자를 운용해야 해
다변수 공식 안에 필수적 조건이 있고—
우리의 운명은 지속적 표면 위에 제한되고
다양한 해결책이 존재한다.

그리고 너와 나 사이의 교집합은
특이점으로 설명되지 않고
그보다는
구불구불한 붉은 실이라,
뒤틀린 포물선이라,
내 평면을 네 평면에 연결하는.

2019.08.10

cosmic inflation

I am but an assemblage of individuating imperfections.
Far from singular,
yet constantly compressed to singularity—
watch me resist and instead expand,
my universe stretches to complete your nightscape.

2019.08.16

우주 팽창

나는 그저 개성 있는 결점의 집합일 뿐.
단수의 개체가 아니지만
끊임없이 특이성을 향해 압축되는—
내가 저항하다가 확장하는 걸 지켜보아라,
내 우주는 너의 밤하늘을 완성하기 위해 늘어난다.

2019.08.10

befriending shadows

If I dared to slice my essence open,
my body from my soul, split to expose
a heart with shadows lounging deep within,
blinding, though the darkness in it grows—
then could I stop squinting to acknowledge
the friends before me (sickly though they be)?
Greet them by name so I may now move forward,
untethered, humbled, broken, bare but free.

2019.08.20

그늘과 친해지기

내 본질을 갈라서 열어 보일 용기가 있다면
내 몸을 내 영혼에서 갈라내어 보여준다면
그림자가 깊게 드리운 심장이 있을 테고
눈 앞을 가리지만 그 안의 어둠은 자라나겠지—
그러면 나는 드디어 눈을 똑바로 떠서
앞의 벗들을 인정하게 될까 (그들이 아무리 병약해도)?
그들의 이름을 부르며 인사해, 내가 이제는 진전할 수 있게
매이지 않고 초라하고 깨지고 헐벗었지만, 자유로운 채로.

2019.08.20

counting sheep

Someone once asked, "What's in a name?"
But I want to know,
what's in a number?
Some days I count my blessings alongside my sorrows,
like sheep at night,
but if 1 is worth 99,
what then does magnitude matter?
A flock is just a fragment by another measure.

2019.11.04

양을 세다

누군가 물었다: "이름이 별거니?"
하지만 난 묻고 싶다,
숫자가 별거니?
어떤 날은 내 걱정과 축복을 동시에 계수하니
마치 밤의 양 같구나
하지만 1이 99만큼의 가치를 지닌다면
규모가 의미 있을까?
한 무리는 척도에 따라서 그저 단편이기도 하다.

2019.08.20

carrying joy

I placed her on a pedestal,
That Joy my heart did crave,
Then quickly tried to topple it,
Lest I become her slave.

My stunted arms derided me,
My reach a paltry grasp,
An idol would that Joy become
Should I not bring her back.

Though crueler masters doth exist,
Than Joy perched on a throne,
Mere backs weren't made to bear the weight
Of lords and burdens both.

The irony of straining to
Remove a crown I placed;
The ruler etched her reign on me
And cannot be erased.

To wait for Joy to abdicate
Dares Grief to overthrow,
For power begs a monarch
Command the heavy load.

So how do I dismantle it—
A void that must be filled,
A seat that I did authorise,
Commissioned, built, and willed?

기쁨을 지니다

난 그녀를 높이 세웠다
내 마음이 원한 기쁨을,
급히 무너뜨리려던 심정은
그녀의 노예가 되기는 싫은.

내 팔은 저해되고 날 비웃었고
내 손이 닿지 못하는 거리네,
그 기쁨이 우상 될 위기에 처해
나 그녀를 돌려내지 못할 시에.

더 잔인한 주인 물론 존재하지
왕좌 위에 앉은 기쁨보다야,
미천한 등에 그래도 버거워
주인과 부담을 합친 것 마냥.

아이러니하게 난 발버둥 쳐
손수 씌운 왕관을 치우려 해;
통치자의 통치 내게 각인했고
그것은 지울 수 없는 것이네.

기쁨의 퇴위를 기다리는 건
슬픔이 타도하길 기대한 것,
권력이란 군주의 책임 만드네
과부하를 지휘하는 법.

어떻게 정리를 해야만 할까—
채워야 하는 빈 곳이지
한때 내가 허했던 지위의
위임과 제작 모두 나의 의지.

Except perhaps to cedeth to
A weightless worthy Lord,
Who needeth not these human props
To fuel a thirsting sword.

If I could find such Deity,
My Joy need not defend
The plinth that strains to bear her weight
instead becomes my friend.

2019.11.04

유일한 길이란 날 바치는 걸까
짐을 덜어낸 존귀한 주께
이 세상의 디딤돌 필요치 않고
목마른 칼도 아니 휘두를 때.

그런 신을 만날 수만 있다면
내 기쁨은 내려놓겠네 방어를,
그녀의 무게가 버거운 대좌
오히려 내 친구를 자처할 것을.

2019.11.04

a map to mark my soul | 보아스

Grateful to be shattered
by a quick and dirty blow
(did you deliver it, or just permit it?)
when it could have been a slow grind executed by a
dull-toothed saw.

Yes,
shatter me don't sever me.
Dismembered piece by piece—
appendages
are too heavy to be stitched back into place.

So I collect my fragments
beneath the pale moonlight
and grin;
I had never thought of dust as durable before.

I once was clay,
but now,
my gaping gaps are sealed with gold.
I'm a vessel bound by cracks
(they're stronger than stitches);
marked by a thumb
with a golden map—
and this pattern,
like a fetter,
binds my wandering heart to Thee.

So trace me if you need to
as you wander in the night.
I've found companions by cartography
to be the best at holding hands.

2019.11.16

내 영혼을 표시하기 위한 지도 | 보아스

내가 산산이 조각나서 감사해
무심하고 거친 일격에 의해
(네가 친 거야 아니면 그저 허락한 거야?)
왜냐하면 무딘 톱으로 느리게 썰릴 수도 있었을 테니까.

그래,
날 절단하지 말고 깨부수어 줘.
조각조각 잘린다는 것은—
부속물
다시 하나로 꿰매기엔 너무 무거워.

그래서 난 내 조각들을 모아
창백한 달빛 아래서
그리고 히죽 웃어;
먼지의 내구성이 높다는 걸 처음 알았거든.

나는 한때 진흙이었어,
하지만 지금
나의 쩍 벌어진 틈새는 금으로 메꿔졌다.
균열로 인해 나는 더 촘촘한 그릇이다
(이것은 봉합보다 강하니까);
엄지의 표시인
황금 지도가 있고—
그리고 이 무늬는
사슬 되어
나를 당신께 매었다.

그러니까 필요하다면 날 추적해
네가 밤중을 헤매는 중에.
지도를 제작하며 만나는 동료들이
손을 제일 잘 잡아주는 걸 알았기에.

2019.11.16

outro: come with me

나가며: 나와 함께 가자

terabithia

You toss a rock that dwarfs your hand,
enamoured by the splash
that rains several drops
upon a little pink giraffe
perched nearby;
the Hobbes to your Calvin—
he drinks in the morning,
content to sit,
because boredom has no name here.

We bought our house, in part,
because of this very spot.
So why did I wait so long to bring you here?

My childhood memories are laced with a creek
straddled by a bridge to a wooded sanctuary
where my pen and imagination ran wild.
My dad built that bridge for me
(we should all be so lucky).
The least I could do is build one for you.

Perhaps (one day),
you will tell me the name of your new world.
For now,
I'll just sit
next your little pink giraffe
and, taking a page from his book of wisdom,
make friends with the rain
while I wait for your arm to tire.

2020.08.16

테라비시아

너는 네 손보다 훨씬 큰 돌을 던진다,
풍덩 빠지며
물방울 세례를
근처에 앉은 분홍색 기린 위에
흩뿌리는 것에 너는 매료된다;
너는 캘빈이고 그는 단짝 홉스—
그는 아침부터 그걸 마시고,
흐뭇하게 앉아 있다,
이곳에 지루함 따위란 없기에.

우리가 이 집을 구매한 이유는 한편으로선
바로 이 장소 때문이었다.
그런데 널 왜 이제야 이곳으로 데려왔을까?

내 어릴 적의 추억에 얽힌 건 어떤 개울과
그 위에 걸친 다리와 그 끝에 나무가 우거진 안식처
내 펜과 상상을 자유롭게 펼치던 그곳.
아빠는 그 다리를 나를 위해 지으셨다
(우리 모두에게 이런 복이 있길).
그러니 내가 너를 위해 이 정도는 만들어 주어야지.

어쩌면 (먼 훗날)
너는 네 신세계의 이름을 내게 말해줄지도 몰라.
하지만 지금으로서는
나 그냥 앉아 있을래
너의 자그마한 분홍색 기린 옆에
그리고 그의 지혜로운 책을 본받아서
쏟아지는 비를 반기며
네 팔이 지칠 때까지 기다릴게.

2020.08.16

acknowledgements

Would this book exist had I not stumbled across a Korean boy band by the name of BTS? Likely not—not only because I found myself immersed in an art form that made me want to engage with myself and the world around me once again (thank you Kim Namjoon, Kim Seokjin, Min Yoongi, Jung Hoseok, Park Jimin, Kim Taehyung, and Jeon Jungkook), but also because a mutual love of these artists connected me to some incredible women without whom this endeavour would never have been possible: Ana Clara Ribeiro, a never-ending fountain of encouragement whose big dreams and love of words made me want to dream a little bigger; Kelly Van Houten-King, who constantly reminds me that the personal is always political—I hope to be more like you when I grow up; Wallea Eaglehawk, who believed my words were worth sharing and gave me a platform to do so; Nikola Champlin, whose sexy brain helped me mould my words into something I could be proud of; and Dr. Han Oul, who graciously agreed to translate this work. To my family and friends, thank you for always standing by my side—few of us have perfected the art of grieving, and it means more to me than you know that you gave me permission to do so in such a tangible form.